# Prayer Time

## KEEP PRAYING THROUGH THE STORM

D'Jaydyn Labrun Readus

**author**HOUSE

AuthorHouse™
1663 Liberty Drive
Bloomington, IN 47403
www.authorhouse.com
Phone: 833-262-8899

© 2023 D'Jaydyn Labrun Readus. All rights reserved.

No part of this book may be reproduced, stored in a retrieval system, or transmitted by any means without the written permission of the author.

Published by AuthorHouse 01/16/2023

ISBN: 978-1-7283-7738-4 (sc)
ISBN: 978-1-7283-7739-1 (e)

Print information available on the last page.

Any people depicted in stock imagery provided by Getty Images are models, and such images are being used for illustrative purposes only. Certain stock imagery © Getty Images.

Scripture quotations marked KJV are from the Holy Bible, King James Version (Authorized Version). First published in 1611. Quoted from the KJV Classic Reference Bible, Copyright © 1983 by The Zondervan Corporation.

This book is printed on acid-free paper.

Because of the dynamic nature of the Internet, any web addresses or links contained in this book may have changed since publication and may no longer be valid. The views expressed in this work are solely those of the author and do not necessarily reflect the views of the publisher, and the publisher hereby disclaims any responsibility for them.

# Contents

Opening Prayer ............................................................................ ix
Dedication .................................................................................... xi
Acknowledgements ................................................................... xiii

The Tests   4/18/21 ........................................................................ 1
Its Ok To Let Go   4/19/21 ............................................................ 2
The Protection Of God   4/21/21 .................................................. 3
For Everything There Is A Season   4/22/21 ................................ 4
Don't Be Ignorant   4/24/21 ......................................................... 5
Live   4/26/21 ................................................................................ 6
Sex   4/27/21 ................................................................................. 7
Obedience Is Better Than Sacrifice   5/1/21 ................................ 8
I Press   5/8/21 .............................................................................. 9
I Am Hurt   5/10/21 ................................................................... 10
Drawing Closer To God   5/14/12 ............................................... 11
Walking In The Dark   5/15/21 .................................................. 12
Wage War In Your Situation   5/26/21 ...................................... 13
Choosing God   5/30/21 ............................................................. 14
Trusting God   6/1/21 ................................................................. 15
Still Trusting God   6/4/21 ......................................................... 16
Welcoming God In   6/5/21 ........................................................ 17
Sanctification And Safety   6/6/21 ............................................. 18
Everyone Is Being Blessed But Me   6/26/21 ............................. 19

Gods Love   6/29/21 .................................................................. 20
Jesus Is The Way   7/3/21 ......................................................... 21
The Season Of Heartbreak   7/8/21 ........................................ 22
The Season Of Recovery   7/9/21 ........................................... 23
Love   7/13/21 ............................................................................ 24
The Wait   7/14/21 .................................................................... 25
Victory   7/26/21 ...................................................................... 26
Its Trying To Survive   8/8/21 ................................................ 27
The Present   8/11/21 ............................................................... 28
Be Weary Of The Soul's You Align With   8/19/21 ............. 29
Accept What God Allows   8/23/21 ...................................... 30
Wheres Your Yes   8/24/21 ..................................................... 31
Im Good Either Way   9/5/21 ................................................ 32
Relax And Be A Kid   9/12/21 ............................................... 33
The New Season   9/13/21 ....................................................... 34
You Deserve What You Desire   9/15/21 .............................. 35
A Restful Place   9/18/21 ......................................................... 36
Imperfection In The Flesh   9/21/21 ..................................... 37
Grandmothers Prayer   9/22/21 ............................................. 38
He Can't Hurt You   9/26/21 ................................................. 39
The Reassurance Of God   9/29/21 ....................................... 40
You Can Bare It   10/2/21 ....................................................... 41
Contentment   10/3/21 ............................................................ 42
There's Got To Be Some Rain In Your Life In Order To
Appreciate The Sunshine – Lashun Pace............................. 43
Lord U-Know   10/17/21 ........................................................ 44
Spirit Prayer   10/19/21 ............................................................ 45
Rising Up To Soar   10/20/21 ................................................. 46
The Guidance Of God   10/21/21 ......................................... 47
Focus On Jesus   10/21/21 ....................................................... 48
Giving Myself Permission To Prosper   10/23/21 ............... 49
Praying In Warfare   10/24/21 ................................................ 50
God's Changing My Ranking   10/25/21 ............................. 51
The Perspective Of God   10/29/21 ....................................... 52
A Place Of Unfamiliar   11/1/21 ............................................. 53
They All Are Leaving   11/2/21 .............................................. 54

The Great Release   11/3/21 .................................................................... 55
Continuous Progression   11/4/21 ......................................................... 56
Unequally Yoked   11/6/21 .................................................................... 57
This Is Not The Season For You To Lose Your Faith   11/12/21 .......... 58
What Do You Do When Dreams Die   11/12/21 ................................. 59
A Cousin   11/14/21 ............................................................................... 60
Foregin Lands   11/22/21 ........................................................................61
You Have A Reason To Be Thankful   11/25/21 ..................................... 62
The Joy Of The Lord   11/26/21 ............................................................. 63
This Isnt The End   11/27/21 ................................................................. 64
He Keeps On Doing Great Things For Me   11/29/21 ......................... 65
I'm Coming Out Of Bondage   12/1/21 ................................................ 66
Traveling   12/5/21 ................................................................................. 67
Heal The Wounded Heart   12/6/21 ..................................................... 68
Set Free   12/7/21 ................................................................................... 69
Disappointed   12/16/21 ........................................................................ 70
Narrow Way   12/20/21 ......................................................................... 71
What Do You Do When God Says No   12/28/21 ................................ 72
Stepping Into A New Season   12/29/21 ............................................... 73
Firm Foundation   12/30/21 ..................................................................74
This Is The Beginning Of A Success Story   1/1/22............................... 75
I Know The Lord Will   1/3/22 .............................................................. 76
Having A Moment   1/9/22 .................................................................... 77
Success And Progress   1/14/22 .............................................................. 78
When This War Is Over   1/19/22 .......................................................... 79
Im Going To Wait On You   1/25/22 ..................................................... 80
Your Name Is In Places Your Feet Have Yet To Tread   1/26/22 .......... 81
How Is My Walk With You Father   1/28/22 ........................................ 82
Seeking New   1/31/22 ........................................................................... 83
As Long As I've Got Yeshua   2/6/22 ..................................................... 84
Isolation And Seperation   2/9/22 .......................................................... 85
Trusting God When It Seems Stupid   2/22/22 ..................................... 86
Just Because God Said It   2/28/22 ........................................................ 87
The Season Of Planting   3/1/22 ............................................................ 88
You're Forgiven   3/17/22 ....................................................................... 89
Greater Is The Reward In Heaven   4/3/22 ............................................ 90

| | |
|---|---|
| Be Still And Know He Is God  4/7/22 | 91 |
| I Love Yehweh  4/8/22 | 92 |
| Trusting God To Do The Impossible  4/13/22 | 93 |
| He Lives  4/19/22 | 94 |
| Better Watch Out Yahweh Is Coming Again  5/3/22 | 95 |
| When I Don't Have The Words  5/5/22 | 96 |
| All I Have Is For You  5/24/22 | 97 |
| God Works With Rules And Order  5/26/22 | 98 |
| Why Ask Why  5/27/22 | 99 |
| Don't Rush Your Healing  5/31/22 | 100 |
| People And Seasons  6/9/22 | 101 |
| Going Into Unfamiliar To Obtain Growth  6/13/22 | 102 |
| Stay Calm And Pray  6/15/22 | 103 |
| Let My Tears Speak For Me  6/21/22 | 104 |
| Vulnerable Love  6/29/22 | 105 |
| Lonesome Seasons  7/1/22 | 106 |
| I Need Revival  7/2/22 | 107 |
| The Rough Season  7/3/22 | 108 |
| Hurt People Hurt People  7/5/22 | 109 |
| This Dark World  7/7/22 | 110 |
| The Size Of The Step Is Irrelevant  7/8/22 | 111 |
| This Battle Isnt Yours  7/13/22 | 112 |
| Youre Never Alone  7/16/22 | 113 |
| The Revealing Season  7/17/22 | 114 |
| God's Going To Repay You  7/17/22 | 115 |
| The Next Season  7/25/22 | 116 |
| The Center Of My Joy  8/2/22 | 117 |
| Decisions  8/9/22 | 118 |
| When You Sit In The Dark To Long  8/11/22 | 119 |
| Love Don't Change  8/23/22 | 120 |
| Using Your Authority  8/28/22 | 121 |
| Evolution  8/31/22 | 122 |
| Don't Look Back  9/1/22 | 123 |
| Consistency And Contentment  9/8/22 | 124 |
| | |
| The Conclusion  1/6/23 | 125 |

# Opening Prayer

Firstly God, I want to thank you simply for this great opportunity, thank you for trusting me enough with this task and helping me to complete it all the way to the end. God, I pray this book helps someone get what they need from you in whatever circumstances they may find themselves in at any point of their lives. God, I ask a fresh dose of purification to fall fresh on the reader God, I ask you to cleanse them from the inside out and forgive them for any sin they've committed thus far. God walk beside them in these last and evil days, teach them right from wrong and give them a praying spirit to help them to last. God, I thank you for the reader guide them as they read this book speak to them like only you can, give them clarification on what it is you had me to write in these pages, and God, we'll forever give you all the glory and honor that is due to your most holy and righteous name. Thank You God Amen.

For a moment worship the God of Abraham, Isaac, Jacob, and Brun Readus.

# Dedication

I'd like to dedicate this book to these two vivacious women:

Firstly, to the late great Barbara Gene Taylor-Readus. I simply want to say thank you. Our time together seemingly was very short, but I thank God for the time we did have I thank you for the many lessons that stayed with me down through the years, it's because of you that I am where I am today, thank you for being a praying woman and never ceasing, I will always love you.

Secondly, to the late great Lizzie Mae Moore Turner. Thank you for being my best friend for 15 amazing years, the highlights of my life were the times we spent together, and I miss that every single day. Thank you for your tender love and care you'll never be forgotten. I'll always love you.

# Acknowledgements

I would like to give a huge thank you to first my best friend, God the Almighty one for every hard time, for every disappointment, for every tear, for every laugh, for every goodtime, and for every blessing best friend I say thank you. Then to my parents I want to thank you for always being there, always guiding and always protecting you've done an amazing job if I do say so myself. To my siblings (Zari, Nicholas, Patrick, Trinity) thank you for always supplying the need, also for being there for me in many of my darkest moments everything each of you have done to make an impact on me is greatly appreciated and I love y'all for it. To Auntie Kym, Ke'Sia and Sha'Maya I simply want to say thank you, thank you for the years of guidance and lessons they will stay with me all my days. Each of you have sown into my life in many ways and I'm forever grateful. To my leaders (Pastor M.A. Pace and Reverend Virdell Lewis) I thank God every day for the leadership of you both. Knowing that I've been blessed with two leaders that I could come to at any time has always been a calming feeling. God placed you both in my life for a reason and I appreciate you both every day for your wonderful impact and your excellent leadership. To my heart (Caila McKinley) they say if your ever fortunate enough to get one true friend try your best to hold on to them because true friends are hard to find. God blessed me with you way back in sixth grade and I had no idea that he would use you to be one of my main support systems while writing this book, but I thank you for always being there and being supportive and always keeping me on task, Gods has his very best waiting on you just keep pushing. To all my other family and friends thank you for you everlasting love, they say it takes a village to raise a child and I thank God every day for my village. Then to my auntie (Lydia Pace) one day you said "Get a journal and start writing what God is giving you while you're praying and meditating on his word" I took your advice and went out and bought a journal, I had written about 10-20 pages when the Lord spoke to me saying you're going to turn this into a book. As shocked as I was, I went on with the guidance of God. You never know how God will use you, but I want to thank you for every prayer you've prayed for every encouraging word and for every song. I appreciate your impact on my life and I'll always love you for it.

    Lastly to the reader, I pray this book can help you in whatever situation you're facing right now or any situation you may find yourself in the future. Always remember to pray and never faint.

# The Tests 4/18/21

We've all had the privilege to experience one or two of God's tests. Let me tell you a little about what I learned about the tests of God. God will test you to see do you really know him at his word. No matter what a person tells you or what you've seen in your life God always tests you to see will you hold on to his word. Beloved sometimes the tests of God can get challenging, but you must remain humble and know that you're not in the battle alone. Learn to thrill to God's word and when tests do come you will know how to stand. Don't let any individual turn you against God with their swift words. Just because God is testing you doesn't mean he's forsaken you. Keep standing Beloved. Take the test as a learning experience because surely its only building you into a better person.

# Its Ok To Let Go 4/19/21

---

Beloved I want to express to you that its ok to leave it alone. Some of us are in spaces needing to forgive others to move on with our lives. While others are needing to let go of certain people, but whatever your situation may be beloved. Be ok with letting go of whatever it is, God wants you to know that the pain and hurt and heartache or disappointment you're holding on to is only weighing you down. God wants you to fly high but your carrying extra baggage. (1 peter 5:7) God is in position to carry that weight for you just give it over to him and let it go. The sooner you let go the sooner you can move on to what God has planned for you. You shall have whatever it is you say, speak your healing and speak your deliverance. God is in position!

# The Protection Of God   4/21/21

My simple pray is Father put a barrier of protection around us, God help us to seek you and to have faith in you daily. Lord its already done thank you for protecting me. It is very important that we pray for protection in these last and evil days the scripture tells us the enemy is on the prowl seeking for whom he can devour so saints we must stay prayed up. God is in position to protect you from any hurt harm or danger. Ask him to wrap his loving arms around you and hold you close. This is my prayer for you a prayer of sincere protection.

# For Everything There Is A Season  4/22/21

God help me to walk in my season, help me to pray your will into my life every day. I want everything you have for me. Help me to begin my winning season (Ecclesiastes 3:1) Beloved I don't know what you've been praying for, but I want you to know everything has an appointed time. God wants you to know the blessings he has for you will come in their season so I want to encourage you Be not weary in well doing for you shall reap if you faint not, so I tell you this isn't the time to faint but to keep on pursing what God has for you. At the appointed time these things will be added unto you.

# Don't Be Ignorant  4/24/21

Many of us are being tested back-to-back because we are being ignorant. Don't disobey God by not adhering to his word. God is looking at the obedience of his people as well as the sacrifice. Many of us have sacrificed certain things just to build closer relationship with God and I'm sure he's proud of you. But to you that's having a hard time obeying God Pastor M.A. Pace always says your arms are too short to box with God. So beloved humble yourself before the king.

# Live 4/26/21

This season is not the season for you to give in this is not the season for you to succumb to your circumstance or give in to your problems. God told me speak to your mountain and tell it where to go. This is a season of overflow and blessings live in it. It's time to rise and live, there will be plenty of time to die later. Whatever it is God has been calling you to do beloved step out there and live. (Psalm 118:17) (Psalm 37:4) (John 10:10) (Jeremiah 29:11) (Mark 9:23)

# Sex 4/27/21

In today's time sex is one of the most least talked about subjects in the church. I asked God to help me understand what sex really is in the spiritual eye and this is what he gave me. God created marriage for man and women to join as partners and from this marriage the two become one flesh as it says in (mark 10:8) once these two become one flesh they are bond together and expected to ride this thing out until death do them part. In the church or in the household they always told you to wait until marriage, but they never gave you a deep reason on why you should. Nowadays people are having sex with any and everyone and through this you are creating soul ties and that's basically giving that person a part of you to hold forever. Many of us wonder why we can't be what God has called us to be and it's because so many different people are walking around with pieces of you. So beloved even though there are many more reasons on why you should wait until marriage I want you to consider waiting on God to send your husband/wife it's worth it. Prayer takes a deep part in this process, Praying the temptation of the devil off you is a hard task but waiting on God and seeking strength in prayer is a great battle strategy.

# Obedience Is Better Than Sacrifice  5/1/21

I want you to understand very plainly that. When God gives you an order the best thing to do is obey. I know sometimes in certain situations we must sacrifice certain things in order to obey what God has asked of us, but Beloved be ok with that. Whatever it is that God is asking you to sacrifice let it Go. God knows the plan he has for you he promised plans to prosper you and not to fill you with evil so stand on that promise. Let go and let God. He notices your obedience beloved.

# I Press  5/8/21

---

On today I had to make the deep commitment to myself that I would keep on pressing, despite my circumstance I would keep on going. In life trials and tribulations can come and sometimes they may seem to damage everything, but God said he's given you the strength to keep going even when you can't see it. Beloved he said you're going to need to reach deep down inside of you and bring up the strength of the soldier and keep on fighting. I know times can be hard, but God will never put more on you than you can bare, and this is Gods promise to you. So beloved keep pressing!

# I Am Hurt 5/10/21

Many times, in life we end up hurting ourselves in multiple ways. The way God showed me was by not obeying what he had told me concerning a thing in my life. God had just spoken to me about obeying what he says and the next week I didn't do that. But many times, when we don't listen to God, we get ourselves hurt or put in dangerous situations sometimes when we fail to consider God in our decisions it turns out bad. So beloved I want to encourage you to always listen to God and let him direct your path He knows the way.

# Drawing Closer To God 5/14/12

While seeking God in prayer time he let me know that I needed to draw closer to him and seek him more. So much is going on in this day in time, but this is no excuse to lose your faith in God in this season we need to grab tighter to God our relationship with God needs to increase, so when the enemy comes in like a flood, we will be able to stand on what God spoke when he said I will lift up a standard against him. When it's all said and done it's your relationship with God that will elevate you. So, beloved get anchored in God.

# Walking In The Dark   5/15/21

In prayer time God help me to realize danger is in the dark and there is danger walking in the dark. God gave me this for those of you that are just in the world going on about your daily lives not taking any time to thank the creator for all he's done for you this page is for the prayer less saints and the backsliders. I want to express to you that you're in danger your life might be full of earthly sunshine but in the spiritual realm you're walking in the dark. Beloveds establish a relationship with God today let him save you from the darkness that you didn't realize you were in. God is in position to take you in as his own allow him into your heart ITS ALL WORTH IT! No more darkness.

# Wage War In Your Situation 5/26/21

In this space I found myself in I thought the devil was going to defeat me in my warfare. But God whispered to me wage war against him. We as the people of God are tired of the devils' tricks and schemes so God told me to wage war against the devil. If your tired of him messing with your peace, joy, or your happiness wage war on him. And use the intrinsic weapons God has given you beloved your weapons are not carnal but MIGHTY. BELIEVE IT

# Choosing God   5/30/21

My simple prayer for today is God, I choose you in every situation in every circumstance through the pain and the disappointment through the joy and the laughter I choose you. Lord you are the head in my life now help me to live in my royal status. Lord, I pray your will into my life, and it is so amen. Beloveds apply this prayer to your life. In some situations God is just waiting on you to choose him over everything.

# Trusting God   6/1/21

Beloved we must continue to trust God no matter how hard the situation maybe, be no matter what the devil throws your way. You must continue to trust in the lord with all your heart. Obstacles in life get rough and sometimes you might think they won't ever end but I know a comforter! Let him grab you during your circumstance and hold you close. He wants to protect you, but you must first trust him. Trusting him means letting go of all your doubts and all your worries and believing him to make a way for you regardless of what you're going through. Trusting him build your faith.

# Still Trusting God  6/4/21

My prayer of today is God help me to keep trusting in you. I know we can say oh God, I trust you but sometimes we must bring some reassurance to the table after coming out of the fire and the flood I'm telling God no matter what's ahead I'm still going to trust you. No matter the Good, the bad, the happy or the sad I'm going to trust in you. So, God help me to continue building my faith in you and to acknowledge you as my tour guide through this thing called life!

# Welcoming God In  6/5/21

Beloved, God wants you to know that the problem your facing can be solved all you have to do is invite him in. By inviting God in your telling him I need you, I want you, I got to have you There is no other way around it. God could come in the midst of your situation if he wanted to anyway but most times all he wants us to do is ask him to come in and abide there. His in position to change your situation.

# Sanctification And Safety   6/6/21

---

We lose our sanctification searching for safety by leaning on our own understanding. When God gave me this I immediately thought of the children of Israel. God had brought them out of Egypt, and he promised them that he would provide a land overflowing with milk and honey. But while they were going through the wilderness a lot of things happened and the children of Israel lost their trust in God and by doing this, they leaned on their own understanding which ultimately got them in a bad position. God is telling you he promised you to provide so all you must do is hold on to what he said to you. Hold on and trust God through this

# Everyone Is Being Blessed But Me   6/26/21

Beloved sometimes we find ourselves in spaces where we realize that everyone around us is in their season of bloom and overflow and yet here, I am in this place praying fervently and I'm not being blessed. I found myself in the place once and after asking God what to do when I'm here God told me. Prepare, we must realize that God is going to do it at the appointed time so while you're in the waiting stage God said prepare for your season of bloom. So beloved if you ever find yourself here, I want you to PREPARE!

# Gods Love    6/29/21

God loves us more than anything or anyone through your faults, God still loves you. Many of us are searching for love from people and they keep breaking our hearts or letting us down. God said until you search for love where its unlimited you will continue to hurt yourself. God's love for you is so strong that he wants to protect you from everything that comes to try to destroy you. Beloved I want you to grab ahold to Gods undying love it's much better than what you're searching for in people.

# Jesus Is The Way   7/3/21

This page is specifically for those who need guidance. Beloved we need guidance in this day in time. God wants you to know that Jesus is the way. In your prayer time develop the prayer God guide me to where I'm needed to go. Jesus is in position beloved to carry and guide you all you must do is grab ahold of his hand right now as your reading grab Gods hand and tell him "Wherever you lead me ill follow" even when times get tough God help my strength to never fail! Beloved Jesus is the way.

# The Season Of Heartbreak 7/8/21

Here we are in this season. The season of heartbreak I know that most of us have found ourselves heartbroken by anything from people to circumstances. But to you that is in this place right now God wants you to know that he knows that your broken and hurt but beloved let him raise you up from that place of blackness. Beloved let God be your very present help in this time of trouble. I want you to know that weeping may endure for a night, but joy will come in the morning. So even though your heartbroken God wants you to know that there's a great revival coming for you. Restoration is on the way!

# The Season Of Recovery   7/9/21

After your season of heartbreak look to God to reconstruct you into the person, he wants you to be. God wants you to be the best version of yourself you can be. Sometimes the enemy will make us think that God is punishing us because of the bad things that happen in our lives, but beloved bad things only come to make you stronger, and God is in place to help you recover from that situation. Beloved you are stronger than you think, and I want you to know, God is reconstructing you, if you allow him and trust him to bring you through.

## Love   7/13/21

God wants us to remember that in all ways we need to love. God told me remember I made you in love so go out and show someone else the love of God in you. But always Guard your heart learn to display love in every way. God loves you so go out and love someone else. This day in time the world needs love pure love. God's love for you is undying and compassionate. Beloved if you are needing love and searching for it, I want you to come to God. Let God love you better than any human can let him surround you in his love. He's in position to do so.

# The Wait    7/14/21

God never designed his children to get everything we asked for right when we ask for it. When God wants you to have something and its major or life changing. He's going to make you wait for it and in most cases the wait is only in place to mature you. Through the wait there will be some things we are going to face so the wait can be worth it. Beloved keep waiting on God for at the appointed time he will do it!

# Victory    7/26/21

Beloved I want to tell you very stern get up and claim the victory over your life. Get up and tell the enemy enough is enough I am tired of you playing with my emotions and you must go. If your sick tells the devil I claim my victory in my situation. Most times the reason why we don't come out victorious is because we don't claim authority in our battles. If I can position you to a place where you can claim your victory before the battle is over beloved your whole life will be changed. Get this new skill in your brain when you're in warfare victory is yours.

# Its Trying To Survive  8/8/21

One summer I decided I was going to start my own garden I spent hours tending to that garden before anything sprouted up. One morning I saw a squirrel digging in my garden that I had just planted seeds in and upon seeing him I automatically thought he's ruining what I've worked so hard for. So, I ended up shooting him he passed away. After doing all of this I told my grandmother what had happened and she simple but softly told me "It was just trying to survive" in that very moment I didn't consider that the squirrel maybe was trying to feed himself or maybe its family. Many times, we are so quick to destroy, and we don't look at situations how we need to. So, beloved make sure to take a second look at things before you make a decisions examine hard on the things you worked for. Your decision could be fatal.

# The Present    8/11/21

God has designed us to live in this present time, beloved God has a lot in store for you in this season of present. Through all the good and all the bad God still has a plan for your present time. I want to prophesy to you that your present time isn't in vain to anyone who is going through anything your pain and sorrow has a purpose behind it. Pray the prayer my present time has purpose and let's believe God for deliverance Beloved.

# Be Weary Of The Soul's You Align With  8/19/21

---

We as the people of God have a specific people we should always dwell around. One rotten apple can ruin the whole bunch. When we align with people who have no desire to live in the same righteous principles as us, we can fall into sin or do the things unrighteous people do. In some cases, Jesus had to dwell around people who weren't holy to get them saved. If your around unrighteous people, make sure it's to bring them to Jesus. Don't let bad people rub off on you your valuable in the eyes of many and God has a plan for you!

# Accept What God Allows   8/23/21

In life we want to ask God questions on why he did this or why he did that but if we can accept Gods will and go on with the things, he has planned our lives will be much better off. I know sometimes we have questions sometimes we don't understand but beloved I want to tell you. You're not meant to understand everything that happens, that's Gods job so the best thing for you to do is accept what has happened or will happen and pray for God to help you move on. Its ok to have questions but try not to question Gods decisions concerning anything in your life or the lives of others.

# Wheres Your Yes  8/24/21

God helped me realize there might be only one thing stopping you from getting those things God wants you to have or the one thing you have been praying for and that is a yes to the lord. Most of us don't understand how important a yes to God is, he wants you to surrender to his will and say yes to everything he has coming your way. Some of you have been praying for years needing God to do something and you have failed to give him a "yes" Beloved give God a "yes" on today in your prayer time give it to him.

# I'm Good Either Way 9/5/21

You must know beloved that no matter the outcome of your situation you're going to be good. If it goes left or right or up or down, you're going to be alright. Beloved I want you to know that Gods got you (Romans 8:28) proclaims that no matter which way it goes it working out for your good so keep striving beloved Gods got this. It's all working out for your good. You might be hurt you might be sad but beloved every pain every heartbreak every disappointment every setback every tear it's all working for your good. SONG: MY TIMES – LaShun Pace

# Relax And Be A Kid 9/12/21

Sometimes we get so wrapped up in the responsibilities or the duties that come with growing up or getting older that we don't take the time to relax and take a load off working has sometimes killed us, but I want you to make sure that you make time to relax. Many of you are over working yourselves beloved taking a load off and enjoying your time its essential to your mental, physical, and spiritual health.

# The New Season  9/13/21

Beloved I can't express to you how excited I am about this new season God is about to deliver you into after going through so much these last few days, months, or years whatever your situation might be God said its done and a new season is on the way. Currently in my life. I had to pray fervently and after seeking God this is what he gave me. So, to you I know your new season might not be at the same exact time as mine, but I want you to declare its coming. This is an affirmation and a prayer for your life.

# You Deserve What You Desire   9/15/21

To the angelic people walking around Gods earth. Those of you that are always helping others, being kind etc. I want you to know that God said you deserve what you desire in every situation. We all have our own desires and wants, and God wants you to know that you desire those things so don't you ever settle for anything short of the best of your desires. Many times, we as the people of God settle for everything but the best but I want to remind you that your father in heaven wants nothing but the best for you so go after it beloved.

# A Restful Place  9/18/21

Sometimes we modern day people need a break. We need to rest a minute from our everyday trials. God said all he needs you to do is get in his presence and in his presence, you will find the joy, peace, happiness, love, and everything else that you have been looking for. I want you to rest in his presence let him fill your needs and take the burdens off your shoulders. In life we forget that we can carry our burdens to the lord and rest in his presence. So, in your prayer time I want you to get into a restful place.

# Imperfection In The Flesh 9/21/21

Beloved when we do things displeasing to God, we move ourselves further into imperfection. Once we get the motivation to let go of all our imperfection then we will be able to be made perfect in the sight of God. Throughout our lives we have done so much and many times God has been trying to call us out of these things I call imperfection. Beloved I want you to know that God wants you to be made perfect in his sight. Let go of any imperfection.

# Grandmothers Prayer 9/22/21

My grandmother has been gone for 10 years now and I have realized that it's a grandmother's prayer that Keeps us going from day to day. Grandmother held the family together. So, to you that have grandmothers show them as much love and care as you can while you still have them because many have lost their grandmothers. And to you women who will one day become grandmothers make sure you keep your children and grandchildren in prayer. A grandmother's prayer is the most fervent for her family. Therefore, the woman is the backbone of the family. I know there are many kids out there today who are missing their grandmothers but beloved I want to encourage you to make Grandma proud. Change the world with her in mind.

IN MEMORY OF: BARBARA GENE TAYLOR-READUS

# He Can't Hurt You 9/26/21

St Luke 10:19 declares that nothing can hurt you. God tells us that he has given us the power to tread upon demonic things all things that are trying to destroy you, beloved it can't hurt you. That scripture goes on to say that nothing by any means shall harm you, so you take your power and use it against the enemy in your warfare. Walk in truth and in boldness knowing that God said nothing can hurt me so no matter what you're going through I want you to know that if you declare this scripture in your prayer time. God said it shall come to pass for you.

# The Reassurance Of God  9/29/21

The scripture tells us God is not a man that he should lie neither the son of man that he should repent. So those things that God has spoken Concerning you and yours's believe me that's your reassurance if you're in a place thinking God has forsaken you the scripture gives us all the reassurance we will ever need. I know sometimes we as modern people get tired of waiting on God and God is so patient and we get to thinking "God are you still going to do it for me" and God wants you to know that you have reassurance.

# You Can Bare It 10/2/21

I want to tell you that no matter where life gets you in whatever tribulation you face you must remember that you can face your adversity. God promised that he would never put more on you than you can bare so beloved stay grounded this battle isn't going to take you out continue to hold on to God. If God allowed the battle to come into your life surely you can conquer it. Life has many ups and down and the troubles of life can make us seem like we can't win. But beloved the weapons of your warfare are not carnal but mighty believe it!

# Contentment   10/3/21

---

Beloved you must know and realize that you have to be content in every aspect or situation of your life. Philippians 4:11-13 You must be content beloved no matter what happens in your life no matter who walks in or out. No matter if your rich or poor. You must remain content with what God has allowed in your life. I found myself being far more blessed by thanking God for what I have and be ok with not being the richest man or having the biggest house. But thanking God for everything that he has given. Despite life's circumstances beloved be content. Somebody wants what you have!

# There's Got To Be Some Rain In Your Life In Order To Appreciate The Sunshine – Lashun Pace

We must go through troubled times in order for us to realize how good God has been to us. God takes us through storms and floods every now and then so that you won't forget that despite what I'm going through better is the end of a thing and my later days will be greater. So beloved if you're going through some rainy days be glad because trouble doesn't last always. Look forward to the sunshine after the rain. Pray the prayer trouble doesn't last always.

# Lord U-Know     10/17/21

Beloved I want you to know that God knows. He sees you where you are, and he knows what you're Going through. He said I have surely seen the afflictions of my people and I have heard their cry. I want to encourage you to continue to wait on the lord for in due time he will renew your strength. God said he is watching over you he sees those secret places. Cry out to God and let him heal the hole in your soul. He knows so hang on in there.

# Spirit Prayer 10/19/21

We must learn to always pray in the spirit. On this day I had to seek God early this morning praying in this spirit because God has pushed me to pray for those who aren't saved. Praying in the spirit breaks strong holds, so if you're in need of a breakthrough make sure you're praying in the spirit. I am aware that there are different levels to praying and many don't know how to pray in the spirit. So beloved ask God to intensify your prayer life ask him to take you higher in your prayer time. In this day in age, we have to prayer more and worry less. Spirit prayer breaks chains tears down demonic kingdoms brings down demonic forces and most of all it strengthens the warrior of God.

# Rising Up To Soar   10/20/21

There's a book out entitled "Rising up to soar" by Carmen A. Smith. Through reading this book God told me to rise and soar like the eagle in the sky. God wants you to know beloved that whatever your circumstance is it can't by any means hurt you ST LUKE 10:14 proclaims it and I tell you beloved that I believe Gods word, so I want to encourage you to rise and soar. Your situation cannot hold you hostage for ever. I speak strength to you.

# The Guidance Of God 10/21/21

God has the plan just follow. Beloved you need to know that Gods guidance is the best. Sometimes we try to direct our own path and we forget that God made the path. We need to make the effort to seek God in prayer for guidance in every step we make. God is there with you to guide you through that situation that might seem so difficult to face. But God knows the plan he knows the way in, and the way out let him guide you!

# Focus On Jesus    10/21/21

---

I don't know who this is for, but God told me that I can't get to the next space of my life until I rid myself of all distractions, people, job troubles, objects ETC. I'm reminded of when peter was out on the water, and he began to look at all the waves and the fishes beneath his feet and peter lost focus on Jesus and he began to sink. Some of you are sinking and God needs you to regain focus so that he can get you to whatever you've been praying for. That dream job God said focus that dream house God said focus that Godly relationship God said focus any dream or aspiration God said focus.

# Giving Myself Permission To Prosper   10/23/21

Did you know that in life we can stop ourselves from prospering? God has many of us in a season of blessings, but we are too scared to go after what God promised you. If you're starting a business give yourself permission to prosper. You owe it to yourself. The only thing stopping you at this point is you. Give yourself the permission you've needed.

# Praying In Warfare    10/24/21

Beloved it is essential that we pray in warfare in this day in time the enemy is after everything our lives, Children, Parents, Spouses, Businesses etc. The devil wants to wreck everything you have going but to stop this attack we must pray in the spirit and in warfare. We are always in battle make sure your prayer life is strong. The most powerful weapon God has given us is prayer. Many of you don't know the great powers and strength of one prayer. By praying in warfare, you are using the mighty weapon God gave you to prosper.

# God's Changing My Ranking   10/25/21

In this space I found myself in I saw spiritual attacks and much more coming my way. God said I just want to make sure you can stand at this level. I'm moving you up in the spirit God is trying to change some of your rankings, can you stand the test. Times come when God needs for us to move up a level in the spirit. You can go through the basic levels that come with being close with God but at the appointed time you must go up a notch. The situations that are coming you're going to need new weapons and you're going to need training to fight on this level. So, I want you to know that when the battles get harder that's the time when prayer should increase so beware of your ranking. God might be trying to move you up!

# The Perspective Of God 10/29/21

God spoke to me early in the morning with this word. "How do you see your circumstances How do you see your trials and tribulations How do you see yourself". Beloved God said no weapon formed against you shall prosper and you need to stand on that promise. Make sure you change your perspective if you're viewing in the wrong way. Many of us have a disadvantage all because of our perspective on situations if you look at your dreams with a victorious eye that's what shall come to pass if you look at your problems with a victorious eye that's what shall come to pass! Beloved change your perspective and believe God in the middle of it!

# A Place Of Unfamiliar    11/1/21

Beloved many of us have had to step into places that we aren't familiar with for us to get to where God wants us. I know that there are many people stepping into this place today so to the individual that's in this place know that God didn't give you this assignment for no reason stay true to your calling. God has a great plan upon your life. I know stepping into somewhere unfamiliar can be uncomfortable for us but remember there's no glory in the known. This place may be full of pain and suffering but remember that all things work together for the good of them that love the lord!

# They All Are Leaving   11/2/21

I found myself in this place of where everyone was leaving for various reasons from loved ones to friends to partners. I realized that through friends that God will remove anything out of your life that is a distraction to your assignment. Through my time of writing, I lost friends for either decisions I made or for whatever other reasons, but I want you to know its ok to lose people in your journey God is needing you to be free from all distractions or maybe where God is taking you these people aren't meant to go with you. So, in prayer tell God thank you despite how you may feel about the situation.

# The Great Release  11/3/21

At this point in my life, I found myself caught in a crossroad with friends and other people against me. The conclusion of this story ended up in me having to release everyone I thought was my friend. Someone came up to me and said since your loss you seem brighter you seem happier. Beloved God may be trying to get you to release somethings or some people, so I want you to know this is your confirmation to release it. I know life will make you think you have to hold on to things for whatever reasons but sometimes it's better for us to release it. Release can bring so much peace into your life many of you stress over things that you can just release so beloved just release it. Soon it will work out for your good!

# Continuous Progression   11/4/21

---

My prayer of today is God help me to always move forward. Many times, we get in places where we start to move backwards but this isn't the plan of God for us to move back. God wants you to always prosper he wants you to always move forward. So beloved in the midst of life pray this prayer. God fill me with continuous progression!

# Unequally Yoked 11/6/21

In this day in time lots of us face being with people that are unequally yoked, from business partners to friendships to relationships. Beware of partnering with people you aren't equally yoked with. Many of us are trying to grow or move to different spaces in life but there's always a setback with being unequally yoked. You can't expect to move forward as a partnership when one person is less developed than the other. It's important that we ask God who should we partner up with so that our dreams and aspirations will be made with an equal partnership.

# This Is Not The Season For You To Lose Your Faith   11/12/21

Beloved I heard from God on today concerning a situation with a family member God reminded me this is not the season for you to lose your faith. The same God that had me and you way back when is the same God that will continue to keep us so keep the faith. Life throws us different battles and different trails but beloved I say to you despite what life throws at you this is not the season for you to lose your faith. God is in your corner fighting for you. Keep close to God and hold on to him. The circumstances of life might get hard, but God put victory inside of you and because of that we can forever say I am a conqueror so beloved don't lose your faith!

# What Do You Do When Dreams Die   11/12/21

Duranice Pace said it best "What do you do when dreams die" I asked God this exact question many of us have dreamed deep dreams over the years and in some cases, dreams have died but beloved God wants you to know that when your dream's die don't get discouraged. If your dream died beloved apparently it wasn't meant to be. Anything that God has given you and spoken over you shall come to pass. If that dream died it wasn't yours in the first place, but God wants you to know that all you must do is dream another dream. Close your eyes and get before the lord and let him give unto you a new dream. Don't get discouraged dream another dream.

## A Cousin    11/14/21

---

I'm writing this page to express how important it is that important it is that we pray for our family members. Sometimes life can get us so caught up that we forget to pray for our family. Beloved you never know what someone else is going through. I want all my cousins to know that I appreciate every memory every talk I appreciate you for being you. I love you all with the purest of love. Go do great things in this world. Make sure we are praying for our family so many times we get so caught up in praying for everyone else we forget about our family. Let's get on our knees we never know what someone else can be going through.

# Foregin Lands  11/22/21

This is page is specifically for those of you that are lost or in places of unfamiliar. Many of us have been lost and didn't know where we were but God rescued us from the sunken place. So to the lost soul let God rescue you from wherever you are. Life gets hard sometimes, and I know we get in places that are unfamiliar. But beloved stay encouraged continue to press in this season. Despite where you are this foreign place will not take you out. I will not break down before I break through.

# You Have A Reason To Be Thankful  11/25/21

---

This holiday season beloved. I want you to realize you have a reason to be thankful. In many ways despite what happened to you somebody else has it worse. I thank God for all he's done for me because I know that even though I'm down somebody else has it worse. Sometimes in life we start to feel sorry for ourselves and things begin to happen, and we get to think we got it worse than anybody else. But you must realize that you still have a reason to be thankful. Beloveds know that in this season be thankful.

# The Joy Of The Lord   11/26/21

We all have been in places where we feel as if we can't have joy in the midst of our troubles, but beloved God wants you to know "THE JOY OF THE LORD" is your strength. Despite your current situation you can still have joy in the middle of it. God didn't design us to feel like we have to be sad while going through our trails and tribulation. To anyone going through anything I want you to know that the joy of the lord is your strength that's how you're going to make it through. The joy of God is perfect and it's all you'll need to make It through. So, beloved declare this in your prayer time and ask God to fill you with his joy.

# This Isnt The End 11/27/21

You know beloved life gets us in places where situations can be so hard and most times, we just want to call it quits. Yes, I want certain thing but it's too hard. I know many of us have said those statements. God wants you to know this isn't the end. God has two ways of explaining this to me, the first way was your circumstance won't win! The second way is God isn't through blessing you, yes, he sent you a few blessings, but he has way more in store so beloved please don't give up and don't settle because there's more in store!

# He Keeps On Doing Great Things For Me   11/29/21

In every situation I find myself seeing the great works of God, I realized he keeps on doing great things for me. God is elevating us to a new place full of overflow, receive overflow in your prayer time. They always used to say count your blessings and right now I just want to thank God for every one of them because he didn't have to do it. God has done so many great things for me that I know I don't deserve, and I know I'm not the only. So beloved let's give God praise for the bountiful blessings. If God never blesses me again, I still have a reason to praise him! Thank you, God!

# I'm Coming Out Of Bondage 12/1/21

Living in the plan of God is the best place to be. For so long different things have held us down. And we haven't been able to be productive because of the chains that hold us down. But beloved declare "IM COMING OUT OF BONDAGE" these chains aren't going to hold me any longer. I have an assignment from God, and I have to fulfill it. So, beloved ask God to break the chains no matter what they are! God break the chains and set me free.

# Traveling 12/5/21

Hey, I know in the past you have been feeling that you aren't progressing toward anything. But beloved its ok if you aren't moving fast as others but the important thing is your moving. You might be progressing slowly at the moment but beloved your moving! You're not in the same place. Run your own race despite who's in front or behind you. The thing is you're in the race so you're traveling in whatever direction toward whatever God has for you stay in the race and keep traveling! ECCLESIASTES 9:11

# Heal The Wounded Heart   12/6/21

---

I realize and I accept the fact that I'm not the only person going through grief. But for those of you that have had your heart broken by any situation in life, my simple prayer for you is "God heal the wounded heart", In life we take many punches, but I want you to know that you must never be knocked out no matter how hard life gets. In the process right before losing my aunt a song came to me and it wouldn't let me go the song said "I will trust in the lord at all times" God knew what time was coming, Beloved I need you to continue to trust him no matter the force of the punches life throws continue to trust him! God heal the wounded heart.

# Set Free  12/7/21

While reading this page let me declare over your life that you are free from every affliction every setback every doubt every circumstance every trail and every tribulation. Anything that has had you bound beloved I declare that the chains are broken, and you are free rise up and fly like the eagle beloved you are free! Give those problems to God and let him carry them away!

# Disappointed 12/16/21

In this season of my life, I found myself disappointed with a decision God made concerning my aunt. In life we aren't going to always understand every decision God makes and sometimes it hurts to live with decisions he made but we must remain trusting in him, even when the view is gloomy. Despite the pain or grief, we must continue to trust him. In my opinion disappointed is a strong word but it's the only word that embraces the multitude of the sadness I feel. But the question came to me what can you do? And I answered back to myself "Praise Him" yes in my circumstances I may get sad or disappointed, but yet will I trust him. In the end beloved praise will get you through.

# Narrow Way  12/20/21

Saints this road we are on is very narrow, in today's time many people don't want to live a Godly life or walk the righteous walk, but I want you to know that it's important that we remain in God, yes, we fall sometimes but get up and continue to walk. This lifestyle might seem restricting but our reward in heaven will be worth everything we seemingly missed out on.

# What Do You Do When God Says No   12/28/21

The circumstances of life sometimes have us asking God "why didn't you do what I asked of you or why did you say no". But the one real question I realized was what you do when God says no life brings us many different situations that we might not always understand and sometimes God tells us no despite how it will make us feel. But in all reality beloved its best for us to humble ourselves and bow down to his will. The situations in our life we may not always understand but beloved know it is well and we trust these things into the hand of a God who never makes a mistake. God may say no beloved but it's your job to say yes lord. God is looking for your yes.

# Stepping Into A New Season   12/29/21

Y'all, we are stepping over, This page isn't long at all but I want to leave you with a passage of scripture (ISAIAH 43:18-19) Go read it and receive this word. Beloveds go on over into the "NEW" don't look back into the past. This is your new beginning step on into it!

# Firm Foundation 12/30/21

In everything you build, grow, or do. It must be done on a firm foundation. It's important to have a firm foundation for when the floods and the storm come in your life you will be able to remain secure despite what comes your way you can make it. The foundation of God can stand against anything sent to hurt or harm you. Beloved I encourage you to get on a firm foundation! The foundation of God won't ever break or crack it remains steady it remains secure. Storms come but there is a firm foundation for you, Get a hold to it.

# This Is The Beginning Of A Success Story  1/1/22

Walk in truth and walk in the boldness of God beloved because this is your winning season God is rooting for you beloved go after your success story! For every new beginning in your life claim the victory and win!

# I Know The Lord Will 1/3/22

There's an old saying that says "If there's a will there's a way" and I want you to know that the lord will make a way, I know situations might seem impossible to come out of but "I KNOW THE LORD WILL" make a way! You must trust him to make a way he knows the road he knows the plans he knows the way so let him make a way for you!! Trust him to make a way because he will!

# Having A Moment 1/9/22

For those of you going through many seasons of hard times I want you to know that its ok to have a moment, its ok to have a break, its ok to let the tears fall. Take the time you need to ponder on the situations of your life its ok. People will try to tell you that you should be over this by now and tons of other things. But beloved please don't let anyone put a time limit on your sorrow its ok to take a moment to feel however you need to feel.

# Success And Progress   1/14/22

This page is an affirmation I want you all to repeat to yourself and maybe to other's as much as you can, "I'm going to keep moving God has promised me success in this life and I am going to get to it by all means necessary" Beloved in order to progress to success you must keep God first. God said there are different levels of success, and your success won't be like the person's next to you. So don't follow in their footsteps but follow the footsteps of God he has the directions and he promised to make good on his promise. So, watch him fulfill his promise!

# When This War Is Over 1/19/22

Beloved can I challenge you to get excited for a minute about the end of this bittersweet war. Many of us are in various wars but beloved I want you to know the bible says greater is the end of a thing (Ecclesiastes 7:8) God puts certain obstacles in our lives at different time to build us, to shape and mold us. Beloved you may be in a great war right now and the circumstances of life might get heavy but keep fighting I want to decree and declare with sure authority that your current situation will not take you under, but you'll come out victorious with a divine testimony. Keep Fighting

# I'm Going To Wait On You  1/25/22

---

Beloved speaking to you as genuinely as possible I must let you know. Sometimes it's best for us to just wait on God, many times we get tired of waiting for God to do a change or make a huge shift in our lives then we try to do things in our own strength and most times we fail, or situations just get worse. Beloved it's important that we develop a sense of patience when on the journey of obedience and sacrifice to God. You can't do it on our own, whatever you're facing you must wait on God to perform a work. So beloved the wait might get weary, but the best decision is waiting on our God.

# Your Name Is In Places Your Feet Have Yet To Tread   1/26/22

Many of us have desired to make it Big in this world, by going after our dreams. And I want to encourage you beloved I need you to make sure your dreams our fueled by God. When you ask God to plant you in your purpose sometimes we might not like what God has decided to do with our lives but simply knowing that God has set me on this path is all I need to know. Once you get the assurance that God has a set purpose for me, I can confidently say after being planted your dreams and desires will start to grow and flourish. I want you to get to the place where you can say "My name is in places where me feet have yet to trod" Declare some prosperity over yourself beloved.

# How Is My Walk With You Father 1/28/22

What a powerful question to the father, I've made a habit to make sure I ask God this question everyday concerning my everyday life. I understand perfectly that I am human, and I make mistakes and I can't get everything right but, In the effort to be right there's an effort to do right even if I don't get it 100%, I want to make sure I'm still on the right path. In life God will put you in situations where he makes you check yourself on the things you do in life. But by asking God how's my walk with you it shows him that you have the motivation to try and get this thing right whatever it may be that you're struggling with continue to check yourself. God will straighten up your walk afterwhile beloved just continue to do your part.

# Seeking New     1/31/22

I've gotten to the point in my life where I'm tired of seeing the same old things, I'm tired of the same old same old. I want to experience a new thing I want to be in a place of growth and progress. I know I'm not the only one feeling this way. So, I asked God to start me off on this journey and these are the words he spoke to me "Seeking is the action of finding something you desire" so I took that and start off on my journey we all know "If you seek then you will find" so beloved whatever your seeking after seek with joy seek with persistence and I'm sure whatever it is you will find.

# As Long As I've Got Yeshua  2/6/22

God helped me to realize if I've got him the troubles of my life don't matter, the things I go through or the people that walk out don't matter. I feel like sometimes in life we determine our outcome based upon the current situations of our lives (If you didn't get it read it again) God wants you to depend solely upon him in this next season of your life, quit stressing yourself out over things you can't control. As long as you've got him, he's more than the world will ever be. I don't care what your facing God is in control just trust in him, He's got you beloved.

# Isolation And Seperation 2/9/22

On this journey I've discovered God will separate an individual before a major shift is set to take place in one's life. Sometimes its mandatory for us to go into a season of isolation so that we can figure out the pieces to this huge puzzle called life. We can get so heavily distracted by the circumstances in our lives so much that we don't even realize this life changing things God is about to do. Separation is mandatory for many of us so to you in that season of your life where everyone seems to be leaving and your left in isolation God says this is a part of your story so learn in this season. This separation is not by happenstance, but this is a part of your progression.

# Trusting God When It Seems Stupid   2/22/22

Season are going to come where your made to be in a peculiar place where everything God is telling you to do seems absolutely irrelevant to your situation. I've been in places trying to navigate through life under the guidance of God and every turn he was telling me to make seemed so wrong, but beloved God requires obedience not guidance. He knows the way so your response should be "I trust you at all times you know the way I take God" Hold on beloved and trust God.

# Just Because God Said It 2/28/22

I heard LaShun Pace say, "Just Because God Said It That's Enough for Me" So with that being said let me encourage you, God has made many of you promises that he has yet to come through on for various reason but to the discouraged individuals know "JUST BECAUSE GOD SAID IT" it must come to pass for you within due time. I know from personal experience during the waiting season we can get discouraged and we kind of get weary in well doing but beloved continue to wait on the lord he made you a promise and it must come to pass regardless of the trails you may face during this season. Learn to tell the devil to get behind you because he's going to try his best to keep you discouraged but wait on the lord and hold closely to his promise beloved.

# The Season Of Planting   3/1/22

We have arrived at the planting season. Beloved this season is the season for you to bury your seeds and watch them grow and blossom, God said this is your chance to plant the seed in HIS fertile garden and watch you desires and dreams spring forth in due season. Don't miss your chance this season we all are expecting things from God, and he says PLANT THE SEED it's time to make some progress! Plant the seed beloved.

# You're Forgiven  3/17/22

---

Many of us ask God to forgive us for certain things and after asking we go on into our daily lives still carrying these sins, God gave me a vision of a man with bricks on his back walking around all day, this is how many of you are living your lives. You have to understand no matter the depth of the sin if you ask God for forgiveness that sin is wiped away beloved your given a new slate. God's forgiveness is sufficient for each of our lives up unto the day of Jesus's return. So, to that one individual who relates to this page know that you are forgiven, and God loves you through your sins.

# Greater Is The Reward In Heaven 4/3/22

We look for great award and accolades while down here on earth and many times we are here stressing ourselves out about trying to get recognition for things that aren't important beloved work the work of him who hath sent you and don't be concerned with who appreciates you or not as long as you're doing the work of God that's all that matters.

# Be Still And Know He Is God  4/7/22

Beloved God wants to assure you that you can stand in the pain you can stand in the sorrow or whatever your situation may be, you can stand beloved I found myself in a place learning to just simply trust him. When the circumstances of life began to rage, I learned to simply trust him. Because he knows where I am, and he said in his word just be still and know me to be the I am that I am. I learned to stop trying to fix my problems on my own I only make matters worse for myself. Beloved stand still the problems or trials you're facing are NOT too hard for God. Give it to him.

# I Love Yehweh    4/8/22

They say love breaks any stronghold. I've seen myself needing things from God whether it be peace or freedom or deliverance. I later realized that my love for God has gotten me through so many trails in my life. I'm talking about the kind of love that captures you in your faults and comforts you to do better. The kind of love that makes you never long for any other kind of love. God gave me this for those who long for the greatest love of all. So, to you the one who doesn't feel loved beloved he loves you and that more than enough to stand against anything you may ever face, I know you maybe don't feel the love of your family or your loved ones, but beloved God said his love pays for it all so my prayer and declaration is God, I love you. (READ IT AGAIN AND GRAB AHOLD OF HIS LOVE)

# Trusting God To Do The Impossible 4/13/22

While walking outside I heard the Lord say to me "What would you do with one million dollars" I began to name things I would do and how much I would give here or give there. I later realized God was testing my faith, after naming everything I would do with the money I caught myself then I asked God "How would I ever be able to get that kind of money that seems impossible for me" God then replied "Do you trust me to do the impossible" at that very moment I could've fell out in the middle of the street my hands when it up and I worshiped him because in life we as people start to think some things are out of reach for us based off of our current circumstances but because of who my heavenly father is nothing is impossible or out of reach for him. Take that impossible and turn it into possible with the dominion God has given us.

# He Lives    4/19/22

Throughout the days of my life, going through tribulation after tribulation sometimes I had to look back and simply say He Lives, the motivation and support that dwell within those two words give me the strength to keep on going. Because he lives, I can keep striving, because he lives my circumstance won't take me down, because he lives the fear that once lived inside of me is now gone and I can now press forward toward the future. Motivate yourself to keep pressing because he lives. If he made it through you can too, Life is worth living everyday just because he lives inside of me.

# Better Watch Out Yahweh Is Coming Again   5/3/22

You've heard it time and time again throughout your life and here I am simply reminding you again to get your house in order because he's coming again. Coming to do his father's business but my question to you is will you be ready when he returns?

# When I Don't Have The Words   5/5/22

There have been many days that life has simply been beating me down and things just simply weren't going right, I searched for the words that could accommodate how I was feeling but none of them accurately define how I was feeling, but one thing I realized was God knows regardless of if I have the words to express how I'm feeling he knows. Beloved when you're up late at night crying those tears understand that he knows, he sees you where you are, and he knows your situation and one tear is worth a thousand words in the lord's eyes. Sometimes a tear drop and a simple amen is all that's required. Beloved he knows and he sees you.

# All I Have Is For You 5/24/22

My all, everything within me, my strength, my joy, my life, my all is for you. This is a short declaration to God; this is me thanking him for everything he has blessed me with and because of that I say all I have is for you. Beloved we all get to a place in our lives were its necessary for us to dedicate everything back to God, many of you have reach huge milestones and if it hadn't been for the strength of God, you never would've made it. So, on today I say God thank you for all you've given me, and I promise to give my all to you in every way!

# God Works With Rules And Order 5/26/22

Beloved knowing and understanding God's rules is very important on this journey because following God requires you to be structured and submissive. God's rules aren't hard to follow but many don't want their flesh to die and their carefree lifestyles. God's rules are the same today and forever and you must learn to follow them if you hope to live the ultimate life. Once you let go of that sinful life, you'll truly see that God had better for you all you had to do was let go of your will and humbly submit to his. God's waiting to do a great work within your beloved don't let the devil stop you from making it to a wealthy place.

# Why Ask Why   5/27/22

In life situations arise were we don't understand what is happening or why it's happening and many time we go to question God on the decisions he's made, but God told me "why ask why when you know why" I know many times you don't understand why God is doing the things he's doing in your life and it might seem like its unnecessary or you feel like there could've been a different outcome, but God wants to reassure you of his word where he said all things work together for your good if you love him and that he has plans to prosper you. So beloved hold on to the word that God has placed before you and know that everything will be alright in the end. Asking why is like questioning Gods decisions I know when we don't agree with God it's hard to not question him, but beloved try your best to just trust him in every situation.

# Don't Rush Your Healing  5/31/22

Many of us have experienced what people call the trials and tribulations of life, these trials and tribulations are somewhat equivalent to a war within depending on your situation but just like any war many walk away with victory but also with wounds. Wounds that are in need of healing, beloved life has given all of us a few scars at different points in time, but because so many of us have simply grown tired of the pain we rush our healing processes, sometimes we pull the scab off before its time and we go back out there with partially healed hearts and seemingly end up making matters worse for ourselves. The healing process is one that should be done slowly and carefully a time where you get to know yourself more and a time where you learn what to do and what not to do in each situation. To you out there who is in this process now beloved take your time while going through this, you're not missing out on anything. Your healing is important for the next stages of your life. HEAL PROPERLY!

# People And Seasons    6/9/22

We all at this point in life have witness the transitions of people and seasons. In one season you have this group of friends and by the time the next season comes many have faded away. The point of this page is to express to you that people change with the seasons and it's not always your fault beloved. Many times, it's not your fault at all people change it's a part of life but what you can't do is continue to hold on to what was, beloved living in the past guarantees no plans for tomorrow. People change with the seasons so it's important we learn the difference between seasonal people and lifetime opportunities.

# Going Into Unfamiliar To Obtain Growth   6/13/22

Beloved life requires us to pass through some pretty unfamiliar place in order to get to where God wants us. Unfamiliar sometimes is uncomfortable but that's all a part of the molding and shaping process God sometimes needs you to get uncomfortable in order for him to do his greatest works within you. I know many of you can testify that it wasn't until you got to your lowest point that the greatest revival came shortly after falling. Growth comes from hard times and that's what places of unfamiliar are places where God has placed you so you could grow. Beloved next time you enter a hard place look at it as a learning experience and nothing else.

# Stay Calm And Pray 6/15/22

To you out there who is struggling with a situation of any kind, someone might've made you mad, or someone could've did you wrong. Whatever the situation might be take a moment to collect yourself and get calm before you make matters worse, pray about the situation and give it to God. I heard Mother Pace say, "Leave it alone, God can handle it better than you can if you leave it alone" So beloved it doesn't matter what they did God will get them for messing with you his chosen treasure. Just don't sin because of the actions of others.

# Let My Tears Speak For Me   6/21/22

There have been many days where life seemingly was getting the best of me, and all I thought I could do was cry. You ever been so hurt that you can't even put words together to adequately express how you're feeling in that moment? That's where I was, I know many of you have had long nights sitting up late crying over certain situations or just the trials of life, but God spoke to me and said "when you can't open your mouth to say how your feeling, your tears tell the story for you" I don't know who maybe has been struggling in life but beloved know that your tears also tell a story. Also remember that God knows what you're going through, and he sees you right where you are.

# Vulnerable Love  6/29/22

Anybody willing to step back out there and take a chance on love. I'm talking to those of you who have been hurt over and over again. Those of you who end up disappointed in those people you thought would be the answer to your prayers. I know how that feels it's called Vulnerable Love the type of love where you're willing to take the risk, but you also don't want to end up hurt again. Beloved God wants you to stop for a minute and seek his everlasting love first before giving your heart to another person. Seeking his love is where you start to actually learn what love truly is, in his love you learn that nothing is impossible, in his love you learn that you're more than enough, in his love you learn that your chosen and unique in your own special way. Seek Gods love, grow in his love learn in his love. Then step back out there and watch how he brings someone just for you. Love looks good on you.

# Lonesome Seasons  7/1/22

These are season many try their best to avoid, because being alone seems too much to bare. But God had to remind me that this is the season where self-love kicks in, this is the season where you learn more about yourself. This is the season where you stop doing any and everything for others, but you start putting yourself first. Many of you are struggling because people decided to leave but beloved it's their loss, use that time to connect with yourself and God its worth it.

# I Need Revival    7/2/22

This is a cry out to God beloved, to those of you out there who simply need rejuvenation God said he's in position ready to put strength and power back into your life. The power you need to finish your assignment, the power you need to break generational curses, the power you need to succeed in this life, God is ready to revive you pray the prayer and let him in.

# The Rough Season 7/3/22

Going through life we all experience that bump in the road, the time in our lives where everything seems to be going wrong. The point in our lives where we are completely overwhelmed, and nothing seems to be helping. I call this the rough season. This season comes most times when you least expect it, and it comes in messing with everything you've established in your life. But to the one out there that's going through this season beloved I want you to know God takes us through rough seasons to build up our inner self or in other words to make us stronger. If rough seasons never came our inner selves would be weak and fragile. But because the enemy is always working God must continue to prepare you for anything the devil may through at you. So, beloved learn in this season it's only a teachable moment.

# Hurt People Hurt People 7/5/22

We all at one point in life have experienced the wrath of a hurting person, regardless of who hurt them or why. In this day in time people don't take the time to heal from the pain they learn to suppress it and go on with wounds that eventually start to bleed on those they encounter. Hurt without healing is a dangerous place for any person, not healing from wounds inflicted on you by those of your past hurt you more than anyone else. Beloved it's important we take the time to fully heal from those scars because even though someone hurt you that doesn't mean its right to pass that hurt and pain onto someone else. And most times we hurt those that care the most about us. Hurt and pain are temporary things not something you have to deal with forever unless you choose to. Make the decision to heal and move forward with life.

# This Dark World 7/7/22

Saints this is a call to pray, so much is happening in this world today many things we thought would never be coming to pass but just as the bible quotes it, sin is on the rise and the devil is busy doing what he does best. Stand there talking about how wicked the world is getting isn't going to change anything. We must get on our knees and pray for our world and even more for our family members. The enemy is out to break up families and pull them away from God. Saints I know we see the changes in the world, but we must pray. To the backslider or the sinner, God knows you by name beloved so what you failed a few times his mercy is sufficient for you. Give your life to him and let him change you from the inside out, he's waiting on you to let go and give it to him.

# The Size Of The Step Is Irrelevant   7/8/22

This page is for the overachiever as well as the overthinker. You out there who has finally decided to get back on track with God and you've made a step in the right direction, but you don't feel your moving fast enough. God said "The size of the step is irrelevant" beloved the simple fact that you made a step is all that matters in due time you'll make it to where you're going but right now move at your own pace God is cheering you on. Just keep moving!

# This Battle Isnt Yours   7/13/22

Beloved stop fighting this battle, give it over to God and let him fight for you. Many times, the devil comes in attacking us and we try to put up our best fight, but God knows the strength of his children and some battle you're going to have to relax on. Because your ill-equipped to fight back against what the enemy may be throwing at you. Its ok to let God fight for you beloved.

# You're Never Alone   7/16/22

---

This goes out to the one who feels left alone, to the one who feels they have no one to turn to. Beloved in my prayer time God called you "His sacred treasure" people may have walked out on you at one point in your life and seemingly left you without a friend. But God wants you to know he will always be there. When you feel you have no one to turn to look to him the everlasting father. I learned a little while ago even when people don't understand my situation God's always there to comfort me In my dark places, all I had to do was reach out.

# The Revealing Season 7/17/22

God had taken me through a season in my life where seemingly everything was going wrong. People were leaving, nothing I did worked out, just everything was going wrong. Later on, down the line God started to reveal to me why things weren't working out and I later found motivation in it. I went through those tough times not for no reason but so God can show me some things. I know there's somebody going through things like this at this moment and I want to encourage you, beloved God is doing a great work stand there and let him do his will later on you'll figure out why.

# God's Going To Repay You  7/17/22

They did you wrong, they might've use you for the unique things you offered them. But beloved I want you to know that God is going to repay you for being so good to them. I know they didn't realize what they had but trust me God will reward you for your efforts to them.

# The Next Season 7/25/22

Beloveds prepare. Prepare for what God has next for you, prepare for what you prayed for. You put in the work you stayed focused, and you followed the timing of God. Now prepare for what you worked for, this next season is for you. Live in the full blessings of the lord, you're set time of favor has come. You deserve this next season.

# The Center Of My Joy 8/2/22

---

He is the center of my joy, when the trials and tribulations of life seem too hard to bare, I'm so glad I can run to someone who can fill me with everlasting joy. The kind of joy that never runs out. Beloved when the days get hard run to the supplier of joy, in his presence is the fullness of joy. So press in his presence and leave all troubles and problems behind you.

# Decisions  8/9/22

Beloved every decision you every make chart out the plan of your life. The road you go down has everything to do with the decisions you make and the end results of your life. I want to express to you that we must take into deep consideration the aftermath of the decisions we make. We have to ask ourselves questions concerning the results of our decisions. We all know someone who has made a horrible decision in their life and now is wishing they could go back and choose the other answer. Beloveds make decisions with knowledge and consideration, Afterall they determine the path of your life.

# When You Sit In The Dark To Long    8/11/22

Beloved when you sit in the darkness to long the light can hurt your vision. Let me explain it sitting in darkness means you're staying suck in a sunken place, a place of now progress, a place of loneliness, a place of solemn and that's just a place where God doesn't need you to be. Trying to get out of that place may hurt your vision because you've been in there so long but how can you find your way out if you can't see. God said "Grab my hand" beloved he's there you don't have to stay in that dark place any longer he's there to rescue you from the hurt and pain you may be experiencing all you have to do is grab his hand and let him lead you on.

# Love Don't Change  8/23/22

Throughout the telescope of time, I've watched people go from supposedly loving me to hating me, as we all have at one point of time. As the season change so do people and one day, I was sitting thinking about it and God spoke to me and said "True love never changed" then I thought about how the scriptures define love (1 Corinthians 13:4-8 "Love is patient and kind; love does not envy or boast; it is not arrogant or rude. It does not insist on its own way; it is not irritable or resentful; it does not rejoice at wrongdoing but rejoices with the truth.") I thought to myself so all those people that left for whatever reason did they really love me? And God said no. Beloved what you have to realize is true and genuine love will never change regardless of what's going on in and around you. True love always remains.

# Using Your Authority 8/28/22

My prayer for you today is God help them to find and use the authority you've given them; God help them to know that power dwells on the inside of them and the situations there going through won't have the victory because if you before use no one can be against us. Beloved I pray you find your authority and learn how to use it. In this day in time using the authority God is given us is a key element to winning this thing called life. Use it God placed it on the inside of you.

# Evolution  8/31/22

―――♒♒♒♒―――

Evolution is inevitable we all change we all gradually develop into either better version of our former selves or worse versions of our former selves. The choice whether you evolve into something good or bad is totally up to you. Evolve in the way God planned you to beloved in his image. He pictures you to be something amazing something valuable. You just have to make the decision to grow in grace and grow in peace.

# Don't Look Back   9/1/22

The song says, "Run on and don't look back, because I'm running for my Jesus, and I can't give up now" Beloved in this next season of your life you can't afford to look back. So much is waiting for you up ahead and looking back is going to cause you to lose focus. I don't know what you may have left behind but trust me if you didn't bring It with you into this next season it isn't important enough to lose focus over. Look forward belove towards the future whatever God has for you, don't lose focus keep your eyes on the prize.

# Consistency And Contentment   9/8/22

For a while I struggled with being consistent with contentment, you know how we are always supposed to be thankful and ok with those things we have and not really be greedy for things we want but don't have. Being content for me was being ok with the circumstances of my life. Yes, others have more than me but I'm grateful that I have what I have. I learned that greed is a trick of the enemy, trying to get you to want something so bad that you actually start to put in the action to get what you want. Regardless of if God wants you to have it yet or not. In Gods timing he will give you those things you desire but you have to stay consistent with being content.

# The Conclusion  1/6/23

Throughout this book I have shared personal experiences and of course my opinion on certain subjects as God gave them to me. I hope and pray that something I went through and learned from helped you grow not only personally but also with my best friend God our heavenly father. I don't know what situation you were in when you first started reading this book, but I pray you came out with the victory. I was asked time and time again what this book is about, and I could never give a straightforward answer. When I first started writing I was writing about what I was going through and how I navigated through that by encouraging myself through what God had given me, but I think this book tells several different stories. It reaches to a variety of different people going through a variety of different circumstances. I think I did a great job and I hope at some point while reading you decided to give your life to God if you didn't now is the perfect opportunity repeat this after me "God I come to you now as vulnerable and humbled as I know how seeking a savior, seeking someone to revive me and I realized you are the perfect person for the job. God, I ask you to come into my heart and to change me from the inside out, I ask you to forgive me for all my sins and wash me in you sons holy and righteous blood. I believe your son died and rose again just for me, so I can be saved. Lord, I commit my life to you even though I may fall help me to always rise with the victory in Yahweh's name I pray amen" and just like that beloved your saved welcome to the body of Christ the angels and heaven are rejoicing. Thank You!